# BABCIA WERA'S POLISH CHRISTMAS COOKBOOK

Homemade Pierogies, Hearty Soups & Traditional Vegetarian Dishes Only Served on Wigilia

HarvestGuard Publications

**Copyright © 2025 by HarvestGuard Publications – All rights reserved.**

No portion of this book may be reproduced in any form without written permission from the publisher or author, except as permitted by U.S. copyright law.

This publication is designed to provide accurate and authoritative information in regard to the subject matter covered. It is sold with the understanding that neither the author nor the publisher is engaged in rendering legal, investment, accounting or other professional services. While the publisher and author have used their best efforts in preparing this book, they make no representations or warranties with respect to the accuracy or completeness of the contents of this book and specifically disclaim any implied warranties of merchantability or fitness for a particular purpose. No warranty may be created or extended by sales representatives or written sales materials. The advice and strategies contained herein may not be suitable for your situation. You should consult with a professional when appropriate. Neither the publisher nor the author shall be liable for any loss of profit or any other commercial damages, including but not limited to special, incidental, consequential, personal, or other damages.

# Contents

Introduction — V

1. Soups (Zupy) — 1
2. Fish Dishes (Ryby) — 7
3. Pierogi & Dumplings — 19
4. Cabbage Dishes (Kapusta) — 27
5. Breads & Baked Goods — 33
6. Cold & Warm Sides / Salads — 39
7. Christmas Desserts (Desery Bożonarodzeniowe) — 45
8. Christmas Drinks — 63
9. Vegetarian Holiday Mains — 71
10. Christmas Cookies (Ciasteczka Świąteczne) — 81
11. Extras & Festive Additions — 91
12. Regional or Oess Common Christmas Dishes — 101

Fullpage image — 108

Conclusion — 109

# INTRODUCTION

Wesołych Świąt, from our family to yours. May your Christmas be filled with love, light, and plenty of pierogi.

But long before we began preparing this book—long before we sat at the kitchen table with timers and notepads, attempting to capture sixty years of culinary wisdom in concrete terms—this journey began as all the best ones do: with the simple desire to keep something sacred alive.

It's easy to lose traditions. One generation misses a step, and suddenly, the knowledge that once lived in a thousand repetitions of hand and heart is reduced to fragments. A flavor you can't replicate. A story you can't quite retell. A holiday that feels hollowed out. That was the quiet fear at the back of our minds as Babcia Wera aged—not that she would stop cooking, but that the soul of her dishes might one day disappear with her. And so, we decided to preserve it. To write it down. To record, as best we could, not just what she made, but how, and why.

When you grow up around someone like Babcia, you think they'll be around forever. There's a strength in her that defies time. Even now, past eighty, her hands move with precision and elegance as she folds dough or shapes cookies or checks a soup for seasoning by scent alone. There's a patience in her rhythm, a kind of prayer in motion, as though every stir, every fold, every slice is part of something larger than food. And it is.

For her, Wigilia is not just a holiday—it is sacred choreography. She begins preparing weeks in advance. The mushrooms are dried and stored. The poppy seeds are ground by hand. The fruit compote is planned meticulously so every dried plum and apple slice is soaked just right. She knows where to shop for each item and when. She has trusted vendors at the market who save her the best cabbage or alert her when the sour rye starter is fresh. And she never, ever rushes.

In watching her, we've learned that the process is as much a part of the magic as the result. The long soaking, the kneading, the cooling, the waiting—it all builds anticipation. It slows time. It gives the season meaning beyond gifts and glitter. It is through this process that we've come to understand that the act of making Wigilia is a kind of love letter—an offering to family, to history, and to the Divine.

Christmas in our home never begins with decorations. It begins with the list. Babcia sits down and writes every dish by hand—each one a non-negotiable presence at the table. Barszcz, pierogi, herring, cabbage rolls, kompot. There's a rhythm to her handwriting, and we've kept some of these handwritten lists folded into the pages of this book like little time capsules. These notes remind us that what she built was never random. It was chosen, year after year, with reverence.

And then, there is the kitchen. As Christmas Eve nears, it transforms. Tables are cleared. Chairs are pushed back. The kitchen becomes a sacred workspace. There is flour in the air and pots on every burner. The radio plays old Polish kolędy, and Babcia hums along, sometimes softly singing the words to "Lulajże Jezuniu" or "Dzisiaj w Betlejem" as she shapes dumplings or braises cabbage. It is a symphony of scent and sound—onions frying, mushrooms simmering, cloves and allspice blooming in hot compote. The house is filled with a warmth that is not just physical but emotional, ancestral.

When I was a child, I remember waking up in December to the scent of sautéing onions and the sight of Babcia standing by the stove in her house dress, a wooden spoon in one hand and a recipe playing out silently in her mind. I didn't know the names of the dishes then—I just knew how they made me feel: safe, loved, part of something bigger. And now, as an adult, I see those same feelings mirrored in the eyes of my own children as they sneak bits of dough or ask, "Can I help, Babcia?"

The answer is always yes. Because for Babcia, the food is important, but the act of sharing it—of passing it on—is sacred. She believes in teaching by doing, in guiding hands rather than giving instructions. She lets the littlest ones stir the poppy seeds. She shows the teenagers how to form perfect pierogi crescents, telling them gently when they've used too much filling. And she lets the grown-ups learn by trial and error, laughing when the dough sticks or the cabbage leaf rips. "No one was born knowing," she says. "You learn by trying."

It's that openness that has kept our tradition alive. Wigilia, as she teaches it, is not rigid. It evolves. We have dishes now that weren't on the table when she was a child. We use tofu instead of fish for our vegetarian friends. We make gluten-free versions of dumplings for those who need them. But the heart of the celebration remains unchanged. The spirit of abundance, the gratitude, the reverence—they are constant.

And it's not just the food that lives in memory. It's the rituals. The hay under the white tablecloth symbolizing the manger. The empty plate set for the unexpected guest reminding us to be open to grace. The first star, spotted in the winter sky, marking the moment the meal can begin. These customs are not elaborate, but they are profound. They ground us. They remind us that this meal is not just a feast—it is a vigil, a celebration of hope, of light in darkness, of peace and promise.

One of my earliest memories is of holding the opłatek in trembling hands, turning to Babcia, and wishing her health and happiness for the year ahead. She broke her piece from mine, kissed my cheek, and said, "Niech ci Bóg błogosławi," —may God bless you. That ritual, repeated each year with every family member, has shaped how I understand love. It is not loud. It is not showy. It is quiet, deliberate, and given freely.

As we gathered these recipes, we realized that each one tells a story. The barszcz recipe is tied to the region of Babcia's youth, where her mother would wake before dawn on Christmas Eve to prepare the beet starter. The mushroom soup is made only with forest mushrooms because, as Babcia says, "It doesn't taste like Christmas if it's not from the forest." The pierogi fillings reflect our evolving family—some filled with sauerkraut and mushroom as in the old days, others sweet with plum or poppy seed for the youngest palates. Each dish has a purpose. Each one holds a memory.

But this book is not just about our memories. It's about yours. It's about the memories you'll make as you use these recipes—whether you are rekindling traditions lost to time, creating new ones, or discovering Polish cuisine for the first time. You don't need to be Polish to feel the magic of Wigilia. You don't need to know how to pronounce every dish or have access to a Polish deli. What you need is a willingness to slow down, to care, and to celebrate the beauty of making something meaningful with your hands.

Cooking is an act of continuity. And through this book, you become part of a lineage—a long line of hands that folded, stirred, seasoned, and served not just to feed, but to connect. Every person who picks up this cookbook continues that line. Every dish made is an echo of Babcia Wera's kitchen and the kitchens that came before hers, going back generations, reaching across oceans and time.

We often talk about heritage as something abstract—flags, names, and ancestry charts. But heritage lives in the pan of sautéed onions. It lives in the steam of boiling pierogi. It lives in the gentle squeeze of a grandparent's hand as they say, "Try this. Tell me if it tastes like home." That's what this book is. A taste of home. A taste of belonging.

So as you read, as you cook, as you share these dishes, know that you are part of our family story now. And we are honored to share this with you. In a world that changes so fast, in a time when so much feels uncertain, there is something profoundly comforting in returning to the same dishes year after year. Something grounding. Something holy.

The kitchen is where we remember. Where we teach. Where we heal. And where we gather not just for the food, but for the love that surrounds it.

In the end, that is what Babcia Wera has taught us more than anything. That cooking is not just about sustenance—it's about presence. It's about showing up for each other. About giving your time, your effort, your care. And in this season of giving, what more beautiful gift is there than to feed someone a meal rooted in tradition and love?

As you turn the pages, as you prepare your own Wigilia table, know that Babcia's spirit is with you. In every dumpling you fold, every cabbage roll you roll tight, every sweet spoonful of kutia, you are honoring a legacy. And you are building one of your own.

Thank you for letting us into your home, into your holiday, into your kitchen. May this book bring you as much comfort, joy, and connection as it has brought us in writing it.

From our hearts and our hands to yours—wesołych świąt. May your home be filled with warmth, your table with abundance, and your hearts with love, today and always.

Chapter One

# Soups (Zupy)

# CZERWONY BARSZCZ

Red beet soup with uszka is a Christmas Eve classic in Poland. Its deep red color symbolizes good fortune and vitality. Traditionally, it's made without meat and served as the first course during Wigilia, often with tiny mushroom-filled dumplings called uszka, meaning "little ears."

 PREP TIME 30 MIN     COOK TIME 1 - 1.5 HRS     SERVINGS 6 - 8

## Ingredients

- 4 large beets, peeled and grated
- 6 cups water
- 1 carrot, peeled and chopped
- 1 parsley root or parsnip, chopped
- 1 onion, peeled and halved
- 2 cloves garlic, crushed
- 2 bay leaves
- 5 whole allspice berries
- 5 whole black peppercorns
- 1 tablespoon vinegar or lemon juice
- Salt and sugar to taste

**For the Uszka**
- 1 ½ cups flour
- 1 egg
- 3 tablespoons warm water
- Pinch of salt
- 1 tablespoon butter (optional)
- 1 cup dried forest mushrooms, soaked and finely chopped
- 1 small onion, finely chopped
- 1 tablespoon butter for sautéing

## Instructions

1. In a large pot, combine beets, water, carrot, parsley root, onion, garlic, bay leaves, allspice, and peppercorns. Simmer gently for about 45 minutes.
2. Strain the liquid and discard solids. Season with vinegar, salt, and sugar to balance sweet and sour.
3. For uszka: Mix flour, egg, salt, and water into a dough. Roll thin, cut small squares.
4. Sauté mushrooms and onion in butter. Cool, then place a small amount in the center of each square. Fold into a triangle, seal edges, then pinch ends together.
5. Boil uszka in salted water until they float. Serve several uszka in each bowl of hot borscht.

**Notes:**
- Storage: Store the soup in an airtight container and refrigerate for up to a week. Barsczc Czerwony can be frozen for up to 3 months

# ZUPA GRZYBOWA

This fragrant Forest Mushroom soup is made from wild mushrooms gathered in Poland's forests, often dried and rehydrated for deep flavor. It's a beloved Christmas Eve option, especially in regions where mushrooms are more popular than beetroot.

 **PREP TIME** 30 MIN   **COOK TIME** 1 - 1.5 HRS   **SERVINGS** 6 - 8

## Ingredients

- 1 cup dried wild mushrooms (porcini preferred)
- 6 cups water
- 1 carrot, sliced
- 1 parsley root or parsnip, sliced
- 1 small celery stalk, chopped
- 1 small onion, chopped
- 2 tablespoons butter
- 1 tablespoon flour
- ½ cup sour cream
- Salt and pepper to taste
- Fresh dill (optional)

## Instructions

1. Soak mushrooms in 2 cups warm water for at least 2 hours or overnight. Reserve soaking liquid.
2. Strain mushrooms, chop finely. Strain the soaking liquid through cheesecloth or a coffee filter to remove grit.
3. In a pot, combine the mushroom soaking liquid, water, chopped mushrooms, carrot, parsley root, celery, and onion. Simmer 45 minutes.
4. In a skillet, melt butter, stir in flour to make a roux. Add to the soup, stir until thickened.
5. Stir in sour cream off the heat. Season with salt, pepper, and garnish with fresh dill if desired.

**Notes:**
- Storage: Store the soup in an airtight container and refrigerate for up to a week. Zupa Grzybowa can be frozen for up to 3 months

# ZUPA RYBNA

A warming Fish Soup made from the heads and bones of carp or other freshwater fish is used for the main dish. Nothing goes to waste—this dish honors the Polish tradition of thrift and flavor during Wigilia.

 **PREP TIME** 30 - 45 MIN   **COOK TIME** 1 - 1.5 HRS   **SERVINGS** 6 - 8

## Ingredients

- 1 pound white fish fillets (carp, cod, or pike)
- Fish head and bones (optional, for stock)
- 6 cups water
- 1 onion, halved
- 1 carrot, sliced
- 1 parsley root, sliced
- 1 celery stalk
- 2 bay leaves
- 5 peppercorns
- Salt to taste
- 2 tablespoons butter
- Chopped fresh parsley for garnish

## Instructions

1. If using fish bones/head, simmer in 6 cups of water with onion, carrot, parsley root, celery, bay leaves, and peppercorns for 40 minutes.
2. Strain broth, discard solids.
3. Cut fish fillets into chunks, and add to the broth. Simmer gently until fish is cooked (10-15 minutes).
4. Season with salt. Add butter for richness.
5. Serve hot with fresh parsley on top.

### Notes:

- Storage: Store the soup in an airtight container and refrigerate for up to a week. Zupa Rybna can be frozen for up to 3 months

# ROSÓŁ Z KURY Z MAKARONEM

This Chicken Noodle Soup is often enjoyed on Christmas Day. This golden broth is Poland's go-to comfort soup. Rosół is believed to cure colds and lift spirits, making it a cozy staple beyond the holidays.

 **PREP TIME** 30 - 45 MIN   **COOK TIME** 2 - 3 HRS   **SERVINGS** 6 - 8

## Ingredients

- 1 whole chicken or 2 pounds chicken parts (with bones)
- 10 cups water
- 2 carrots, sliced
- 1 parsley root, sliced
- 1 onion, halved and charred
- 1 celery stalk
- 2 cloves garlic
- 5 peppercorns
- 1 bay leaf
- Salt to taste
- Fine egg noodles (makaron)
- Fresh parsley for garnish

## Instructions

1. Place chicken in a large pot with water. Bring to boil, skim off foam.
2. Add vegetables, spices, and salt. Reduce heat and simmer uncovered for 2-3 hours.
3. Remove chicken and vegetables. Strain broth through a fine sieve.
4. Cook noodles separately. Shred some chicken for serving.
5. Serve hot broth with noodles and chicken pieces, garnished with parsley.

**Notes:**

- Storage: Store the soup in an airtight container and refrigerate for up to a week. Rosół z Kury z Makaronem can be frozen for up to 3 months

# ZUPA MIGDAŁOWA

This sweet and creamy Almond Soup, once served in noble Polish homes, is made with ground almonds, rice, and milk. A rare but cherished Wigilia starter, it reflects the royal traditions of old Polish Christmas tables.

**PREP TIME** 15 - 20 MIN    **COOK TIME** 20 - 30 MIN    **SERVINGS** 4 - 6

## Ingredients

- ½ cup blanched almonds
- 4 cups milk (or plant-based milk)
- 2 tablespoons honey or sugar
- 1 teaspoon vanilla extract
- Pinch of cinnamon
- Small cooked rice or fine egg noodles (optional)
- Slivered almonds for garnish

## Instructions

1. Grind almonds finely in a food processor.
2. In a saucepan, heat milk gently. Stir in ground almonds, honey/sugar, vanilla, and cinnamon.
3. Simmer gently for 15 minutes, stirring occasionally. Do not boil.
4. Optionally stir in cooked rice or noodles.
5. Serve warm in bowls with a sprinkle of slivered almonds.

**Notes:**

- Storage: Store the soup in an airtight container and refrigerate for up to a week. Zupa Migdałowa can be frozen for up to 3 months

Chapter Two

# Fish Dishes (Ryby)

# KARP SMAŻONY

A Christmas Eve must-have. Fried Carp is often the centerpiece of the Wigilia table. Many Polish families keep the live carp in the bathtub for a day or two before cooking—it's both a tradition and a childhood memory for many!

 **PREP TIME** 30 - 45 MIN    **COOK TIME** 20 -30 MIN    **SERVINGS** 6 - 8

## Ingredients

- 2-3 carp fillets, skin on
- Juice of 1 lemon
- Salt and pepper to taste
- ½ cup flour for dredging
- ½ cup breadcrumbs (optional)
- 2 eggs, beaten (optional)
- Oil or clarified butter for frying

## Instructions

1. Rinse carp and pat dry. Sprinkle with lemon juice, salt, and pepper. Let sit for 15-30 minutes.
2. Dredge in flour (or flour, egg, and breadcrumbs for a crispier crust).
3. Heat oil in a skillet. Fry carp until golden brown and cooked through, about 4-5 minutes per side.
4. Drain on paper towels and serve warm.

**Notes:**

- Storage: Store in an airtight container and refrigerate for up to 3 days. Freeze wrapped individually for up to 1 month.

# KARP W GALARECIE

This elegant Carp in Fish Broth Gelatin dish, served cold, features slices of carp suspended in savory jelly. Though a love-it-or-hate-it item today, it was once considered a gourmet showstopper on festive tables, often garnished with lemon, peas, or carrots.

 **PREP TIME** 40 - 60 MIN      **COOK TIME** 1 - 1.5 HRS      **SERVINGS** 6 - 8

## Ingredients

- 2-3 carp fillets (or whole cleaned carp, sliced)
- 6 cups fish stock (see note)
- 1 onion, sliced
- 1 carrot, sliced
- 1 bay leaf
- 5 peppercorns
- 2 tablespoons vinegar or lemon juice
- 1 tablespoon gelatin
- Salt to taste
- Chopped parsley and lemon slices for garnish

## Instructions

1. Simmer fish in stock with onion, carrot, bay leaf, and peppercorns until cooked (15-20 min).
2. Remove fish and strain broth. Add vinegar or lemon juice. Season with salt.
3. Dissolve gelatin in a bit of warm broth and return to the pot.
4. Arrange fish slices in a serving dish with vegetables. Pour cooled broth over until just covered.
5. Chill several hours until set.

**Notes:**
- Storage: Store in an airtight container and refrigerate for up to 3 days. Freeze wrapped individually for up to 1 month.
- Serve with a squeeze of lemon juice on top.

# KARP PO ŻYDOWSKU

This sweet-and-savory Jewish-Style Carp dish hails from Jewish culinary traditions in Poland. The unexpected blend of raisins, onions, and fish reflects centuries of cultural sharing between Jewish and Polish communities, especially during holiday feasts.

 PREP TIME
40 - 60 MIN

 COOK TIME
1 - 1.5 HRS

 SERVINGS
6 - 8

## Ingredients

- 2-3 carp fillets (or whole cleaned carp, sliced)
- 6 cups fish stock (see note)
- 1 onion, sliced
- 1 carrot, sliced
- 1 bay leaf
- 5 peppercorns
- 2 tablespoons vinegar or lemon juice
- 1 tablespoon gelatin
- Salt to taste
- Chopped parsley and lemon slices for garnish

## Instructions

1. Simmer fish in stock with onion, carrot, bay leaf, and peppercorns until cooked (15-20 min).
2. Remove fish and strain broth. Add vinegar or lemon juice. Season with salt.
3. Dissolve gelatin in a bit of warm broth and return to the pot.
4. Arrange fish slices in a serving dish with vegetables. Pour cooled broth over until just covered.
5. Chill several hours until set.

### Notes:

- Storage: Store in an airtight container and refrigerate for up to 3 days. Freeze wrapped individually for up to 1 month.

# ŚLEDZIE W OLEJU Z CEBULĄ

This simple yet flavorful Herring in Oil with Onion dish is a Christmas Eve classic. Herring is considered a symbol of prosperity, and soaking it in oil preserves it beautifully, making it a staple on holiday appetizer platters.

 **PREP TIME** 15 - 20 MIN    **COOK TIME** NONE    **SERVINGS** 4 - 6

## Ingredients

- 4 salted herring fillets, soaked in water or milk 2-4 hours
- 1 large onion, thinly sliced
- ½ cup neutral oil (sunflower or vegetable)
- 1 bay leaf
- 5 peppercorns
- Optional: a few slices of lemon

## Instructions

1. Rinse soaked herring and pat dry. Cut into bite-sized pieces.
2. Layer in a jar or dish with sliced onion, bay leaf, and peppercorns.
3. Pour oil over to cover. Add lemon if using. Refrigerate 24 hours.

**Notes:**

- Storage: Store in an airtight container and refrigerate for up to 7 days.

# ŚLEDZIE W ŚMIETANIE

**Tangy and creamy, the Herring in Sour Cream version of herring is especially popular in southern Poland. The cool, rich sour cream balances the saltiness of the fish, making it a refreshing start to the meatless Wigilia feast.**

 PREP TIME
15 - 20 MIN

 COOK TIME
NONE

 SERVINGS
4 - 6

## Ingredients

- 4 salted herring fillets, soaked in water or milk for 2 to 4 hours.
- 1 small onion, sliced
- 1 small apple, grated or chopped (optional)
- 1 cup sour cream
- 1 teaspoon mustard (optional)
- Salt and pepper to taste

## Instructions

1. Rinse and cut herring into pieces.
2. In a bowl, mix sour cream with mustard, apple, and onion. Fold in herring.

**Notes:**
- Storage: Store in an airtight container and refrigerate for up to 7 days.

# ŚLEDZIE PO KASZUBSKU

Kaszubian-Style Herring is a beloved Polish dish, especially popular during Christmas Eve (Wigilia). The sweet-and-sour tomato-onion sauce reflects the Kashubian region's love for combining flavors, and herring symbolizes prosperity and good luck in Polish tradition.

 **PREP TIME** 15 - 20 MIN     **COOK TIME** 15 MIN     **SERVINGS** 4

## Ingredients

- 4 salted herring fillets, soaked and cut
- 1 onion, sliced
- 1 tablespoon tomato paste
- 1 tablespoon vinegar
- 1 tablespoon sugar
- ½ teaspoon ground allspice
- 3 tablespoons oil
- Raisins (optional)

## Instructions

1. Sauté onion in oil until soft. Add tomato paste, vinegar, sugar, and allspice. Cook 5 minutes. Add raisins if using.
2. Cool, then layer with herring in a jar. Refrigerate 24 hours.

**Notes:**

- Storage: Store in an airtight container and refrigerate for up to 7 days. Freezing is not recommended.

# ŚLEDZIE Z JABŁKIEM I ŚMIETANĄ

This refreshing dish is called Herring with Sweet Apples and Tangy Sour Cream. It's a great example of Poland's love for balancing sweet, sour, and salty flavors in unexpected yet delicious ways.

 **PREP TIME** 20 - 30 MIN    **COOK TIME** NONE    **SERVINGS** 4

## Ingredients

- 4 soaked herring fillets, chopped
- 1 crisp apple, diced
- ½ small red onion, minced
- ¾ cup sour cream
- Juice of ½ lemon
- Salt and pepper to taste

## Instructions

1. In a bowl, mix sour cream with lemon juice. Fold in apple, onion, and herring. Season.

**Notes:**
- Storage: Store in an airtight container and refrigerate for up to 3 days.

# ŚLEDZIE KORZENNE

These aromatic Spiced Pickled Herring Fillets are marinated with warm spices like cloves, allspice, and bay leaves. Traditionally served during Wigilia, they bring a punch of festive flavor and showcase old-world preservation techniques.

 **PREP TIME** 30 - 40 MIN    **COOK TIME** 10 - 15 MIN    **SERVINGS** 4 - 6

## Ingredients

- 4 soaked herring fillets
- 1 small onion, sliced
- ½ cup vinegar
- ½ cup water
- 1 tablespoon sugar
- 1 bay leaf
- 3 cloves
- 5 allspice berries
- 5 peppercorns

## Instructions

1. Combine vinegar, water, sugar, and spices in a saucepan. Simmer 5 minutes. Cool completely.
2. Layer herring and onions in a jar. Pour marinade over. Refrigerate 24 hours.

**Notes:**

- Storage: Store in an airtight container and refrigerate for up to 7 days.

# ŁOSOŚ PIECZONY Z KOPERKIEM

Though not traditional like carp, Baked Salmon with Dill is a modern favorite on Polish holiday tables. Dill is the star herb here, adding a fresh, aromatic finish that complements the richness of the fish.

 **PREP TIME** 10 - 15 MIN      **COOK TIME** 15 - 20 MIN      **SERVINGS** 4

## Ingredients

- 2 salmon fillets (about 6 oz each)
- 2 tablespoons olive oil or melted butter
- Juice of ½ lemon
- 2 tablespoons fresh dill, chopped (or 1 tsp dried)
- 1 garlic clove, minced (optional)
- Salt and pepper to taste
- Lemon slices and fresh dill sprigs for garnish

## Instructions

1. Preheat oven to 375°F (190°C). Line a baking dish with parchment paper or lightly grease.
2. Pat salmon dry with paper towels. Place in baking dish skin-side down.
3. In a small bowl, mix olive oil or butter, lemon juice, minced garlic (if using), dill, salt, and pepper.
4. Spoon mixture over salmon fillets. Let marinate 10-15 minutes at room temperature.
5. Bake uncovered for 15-18 minutes, or until salmon flakes easily with a fork.
6. Garnish with fresh dill and lemon slices.

**Notes:**
- Storage: Store in an airtight container and refrigerate for 2 to 3 days. Freeze for up to 3 months.

# FILET Z DORSZA SMAŻONY

**Pan-fried Cod Fillets offers a lighter alternative to carp on Wigilia. Its mild flavor makes it a family-friendly favorite, often served simply with lemon or herbs. It's especially popular in coastal regions.**

 PREP TIME
10 - 15 MIN

 COOK TIME
6 - 8 MIN

 SERVINGS
4

## Ingredients

- 2-4 cod fillets (skinless)
- Juice of ½ lemon
- Salt and pepper to taste
- ½ cup flour
- 2 tablespoons butter or oil (for frying)
- Optional: fresh parsley and lemon wedges for serving

## Instructions

1. Rinse and pat dry the cod fillets. Sprinkle with lemon juice, salt, and pepper. Let rest 10-15 minutes.
2. Dredge each fillet lightly in flour on both sides.
3. Heat butter or oil in a skillet over medium heat. Add cod fillets and fry for about 3-4 minutes per side, until golden brown and cooked through.
4. Transfer to paper towels to drain excess oil.

**Notes:**
- Storage: Store in an airtight container and refrigerate for up to 2 days. Freeze for up to 2 months.

## Chapter Three
# Pierogi & Dumplings

# PIEROGI DOUGH

**Polish Pierogi Dough is made from just flour, water, salt, and sometimes egg or oil—simple ingredients that create a soft, elastic texture. The dough is kneaded until smooth, then rolled thin and cut into circles. Its versatility makes it perfect for both savory and sweet fillings, especially during holidays.**

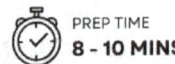 PREP TIME **8 - 10 MINS**   COOK TIME **NONE**   SERVINGS **4 - 6**

## Ingredients

- 3 cups all-purpose flour
- 1 egg
- ¾ cup warm water
- 1 tablespoon vegetable oil or melted butter
- ½ teaspoon salt

## Instructions

1. In a large bowl, mix flour and salt. Make a well in the center, add egg, oil, and warm water.
2. Mix until dough comes together, then knead for 8-10 minutes until smooth and elastic.
3. Cover with a damp cloth or wrap and rest 30 minutes before rolling out.

**Notes:**
- Storage: Store in an airtight container and refrigerate for up to 2 days. Freeze for up to 3 months.

# PIEROGI Z KAPUSTĄ I GRZYBAMI

These classic Wigilia Dumplings combine tangy sauerkraut and forest mushrooms for a deeply savory filling. They're a beloved symbol of Polish holiday comfort food, often made in huge batches as a family bonding tradition.

 **PREP TIME** 1 HR     **COOK TIME** 3 - 5 MINS     **SERVINGS** 6 - 8

## Ingredients

- 2 cups sauerkraut, rinsed and drained
- 1 cup dried mushrooms, soaked and chopped
- 1 onion, finely chopped
- 2 tablespoons oil or butter
- Salt and pepper to taste

## Instructions

1. Sauté onion in butter until golden. Add sauerkraut and mushrooms. Cook 10-15 minutes until soft. Season well.
2. Roll dough thin, cut circles (3 inches). Add 1 teaspoon filling, fold, seal tightly.
3. Boil in salted water until they float. Optional: pan-fry with butter and onions for added flavor.

**Notes:**

- Storage: Store in an airtight container and refrigerate for up to 4 days. Freeze for up to 3 months.

# PIEROGI Z SEREM I ZIEMNIAKAMI

Known as Russian Pierogi, these aren't Russian but actually from the Ruthenian region of eastern Poland. Their creamy potato and cheese filling makes them one of the most universally loved pierogi year-round, not just at Christmas!

 **PREP TIME** 30 MIN   **COOK TIME** 5 - 7 MIN   **SERVINGS** 6 - 8

## Ingredients

- 1 cup mashed potatoes
- 1 cup farmer's cheese or ricotta
- Salt and pepper to taste

## Instructions

1. Mix mashed potatoes with cheese. Season to taste.
2. Fill and form pierogi as above. Boil until floating. Pan-fry if desired.

**Notes:**

- Storage: Store in an airtight container and refrigerate for up to 4 days. Freeze for up to 3 months.
- Use the dough recipe for any pierogis.

# PIEROGI Z SOCZEWICĄ

**Lentil Pierogi add a protein-rich twist to traditional pierogi, often seasoned with garlic, herbs, and onions. They've gained popularity as a hearty vegetarian option for Wigilia, especially among modern plant-based cooks.**

| | | |
|---|---|---|
| **PREP TIME** 25 - 30 MIN | **COOK TIME** 5 - 7 MIN | **SERVINGS** 6 - 8 |

## Ingredients

- 1 cup cooked green or brown lentils
- 1 small onion, finely chopped
- 1 clove garlic, minced
- 1 tablespoon oil
- Salt, pepper, and marjoram to taste

## Instructions

1. Sauté onion and garlic in oil. Add lentils, mash slightly, and season well.
2. Fill and form pierogi as above. Boil in salted water until floating. Optional pan-frying adds extra texture.

**Notes:**

- Storage: Store in an airtight container and refrigerate for up to 4 days. Freeze for up to 3 months.

# PIEROGI ZE SZPINAKIEM I SEREM

A newer addition to the pierogi family is Spinach and Cheese Pierogi. This green-and-creamy combo is as nutritious as it is delicious. Spinach and cheese pierogi are perfect for those who want to mix tradition with a modern, lighter twist.

 **PREP TIME** 20 - 30 MIN    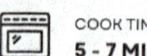 **COOK TIME** 5 - 7 MIN     **SERVINGS** 6 - 8

## Ingredients

- 1 cup cooked spinach, squeezed dry and chopped
- ¾ cup farmer's cheese or feta
- 1 garlic clove, minced (optional)
- Salt and pepper to taste

## Instructions

1. Combine spinach, cheese, garlic, salt, and pepper.
2. Assemble and boil as with other pierogi. Pan-fry if preferred.

**Notes:**

- Storage: Store in an airtight container and refrigerate for up to 4 days. Freeze for up to 3 months.

# USZKA Z GRZYBAMI

**Meaning "little ears," uszka are small dumplings filled with wild mushrooms and traditionally served in barszcz on Christmas Eve. Making them is a labor of love, often passed down through generations of holiday cooks.**

 **PREP TIME** 30 - 40 MIN    **COOK TIME** 3 - 5 MIN    **SERVINGS** 12

## Ingredients

- 1 cup dried wild mushrooms, soaked and finely chopped
- 1 onion, finely chopped
- 1 tablespoon butter
- Salt and pepper to taste

## Instructions

1. Sauté onion and mushrooms in butter until soft. Season.
2. Roll dough very thin, cut into small 1.5-inch squares. Add a small pinch of filling.
3. Fold into triangles, pinch edges, then connect two corners to form a tortellini shape.
4. Boil until floating, about 3 minutes.

**Notes:**

- Storage: Store in an airtight container and refrigerate for up to 3 days. Freeze for up to 2 months.

CHAPTER FOUR

# CABBAGE DISHES (KAPUSTA)

# KAPUSTA Z GROCHEM

**Split Pea Cabbage is a humble dish that is a Wigilia staple, symbolizing unity and prosperity. The creamy peas and tangy cabbage create a comforting contrast, and because it's meatless, it fits perfectly into the Christmas Eve fast.**

 PREP TIME 15 MIN      COOK TIME 1 - 1.5 HRS      SERVINGS 4 - 6

## Ingredients

- 1 cup yellow split peas, rinsed
- 3 cups water
- 2 tablespoons oil or butter
- 1 onion, chopped
- 2 cups sauerkraut, rinsed and chopped
- Salt and pepper to taste

## Instructions

1. Cook split peas in water until soft but not mushy (30-40 minutes). Drain and set aside.
2. Sauté onion in oil until golden. Add sauerkraut and cook 10-15 minutes.
3. Mix in cooked peas, season with salt and pepper. Simmer a few minutes to combine flavors.

**Notes:**

- Storage: Store in an airtight container and refrigerate for up to 4 days. Freeze for up to 3 months.

# KAPUSTA Z GRZYBAMI

Earthy mushrooms and sauerkraut come together in this deeply flavorful vegetarian dish, rooted in forest and field. It's often slow-cooked to let the flavors blend, making it a favorite among traditionalists at the Wigilia table.

 **PREP TIME** 20 MIN    **COOK TIME** 1 - 1.5 HRS    **SERVINGS** 4 - 6

## Ingredients

- 2 cups sauerkraut, rinsed and chopped
- 1 cup dried mushrooms, soaked and chopped
- 1 onion, chopped
- 2 tablespoons oil or butter
- 1 bay leaf
- Salt and pepper to taste

## Instructions

1. Sauté onion in oil until golden. Add mushrooms and cook 5 minutes.
2. Add sauerkraut, bay leaf, and enough water to cover. Simmer 45-60 minutes.
3. Remove bay leaf, season with salt and pepper. Simmer until thickened.

**Notes:**

- Storage: Store in an airtight container and refrigerate for up to 4 days. Freeze for up to 3 months.

# BIGOS WIGILIJNY

Unlike the meat-heavy version served later, this vegetarian bigos is made with sauerkraut, mushrooms, and dried plums. It's rich, tangy, and slightly sweet—a perfect example of how Polish cooks adapt classic dishes for holiday fasting.

 **PREP TIME** 30 MIN  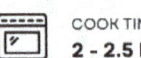 **COOK TIME** 2 - 2.5 HRS   **SERVINGS** 4 - 6

## Ingredients

- 3 cups sauerkraut, rinsed and chopped
- 1 cup fresh cabbage, shredded
- 1 cup dried mushrooms, soaked and chopped
- 1 onion, chopped
- 2 tablespoons oil
- 2 tablespoons tomato paste
- 1 apple, peeled and grated
- 1 bay leaf, 5 allspice berries
- Salt and pepper to taste

## Instructions

1. In a pot, sauté onion in oil. Add mushrooms and cook 5 minutes.
2. Add both cabbages, apple, tomato paste, and spices.
3. Add 1-2 cups water. Simmer uncovered for 1-1.5 hours, stirring occasionally.
4. Remove bay leaf and allspice. Season to taste.

**Notes:**
- Storage: Store in an airtight container and refrigerate for up to 5 days. Freeze for up to 3 months.

# GOŁĄBKI Z KASZĄ I GRZYBAMI

These Meatless Cabbage Rolls are wrapped with love and filled with hearty buckwheat and mushrooms. They reflect Poland's peasant roots and are especially popular on Wigilia for their satisfying, earthy flavor without breaking the Christmas Eve fast.

 **PREP TIME** 45 - 60 MIN　　 **COOK TIME** 60 - 75 MIN　　 **SERVINGS** 6 - 8

## Ingredients

- 1 head white cabbage
- 1 cup buckwheat groats, cooked
- 1 cup dried mushrooms, soaked and chopped
- 1 onion, chopped
- 2 tablespoons oil or butter
- Salt and pepper to taste
- Optional: mushroom broth or tomato sauce for baking

## Instructions

1. Blanch cabbage leaves in boiling water until soft and pliable.
2. Sauté onion and mushrooms in oil. Combine with cooked buckwheat, season well.
3. Place filling in each leaf, roll tightly, tuck sides.
4. Place rolls seam-side down in a baking dish. Pour mushroom broth or light tomato sauce over.
5. Cover and bake at 350°F (175°C) for 45 minutes.

**Notes:**

- Storage: Store in an airtight container and refrigerate for up to 4 days. Freeze for up to 3 months.

Chapter Five

# Breads & Baked Goods

# CHLEB ŻYTNI NA ZAKWASIE

This dense, tangy Sourdough Rye Bread is a Polish staple with ancient roots. Made with natural sourdough starter, it stays fresh for days and symbolizes home, tradition, and nourishment, especially during the cold Christmas season.

 **PREP TIME** 2 - 2.5 HRS    **COOK TIME** 45 - 60 MIN    **SERVINGS** 10 - 12 SLICES

## Ingredients

- 1 cup rye sourdough starter (active)
- 2 cups rye flour
- 1 ½ cups all-purpose flour
- 1 ½ cups warm water
- 1 ½ teaspoons salt
- 1 teaspoon caraway seeds (optional)

## Instructions

1. In a large bowl, combine sourdough starter, warm water, and flours. Mix until combined.
2. Add salt and caraway if using. Knead until a sticky dough forms.
3. Cover and let rise in a warm place for 6-8 hours or overnight.
4. Shape into a loaf and place in a greased loaf pan or proofing basket. Let rise again 1-2 hours.
5. Preheat oven to 425°F (220°C). Score top and bake 40-45 minutes.

**Notes:**
- Storage: Store in an airtight container for up to 4 days. Freeze for up to 3 months.

# BUŁECZKI Z MAKIEM

These sweet Poppy Seed Buns are filled with poppy seed paste, a symbol of abundance in Polish folklore. Eaten during the holidays, they're believed to bring prosperity and good luck in the new year.

**PREP TIME** 2 - 2.5 HRS
**COOK TIME** 15 - 20 MIN
**SERVINGS** 12 SLICES

## Ingredients

- 2 ½ cups all-purpose flour
- ½ cup warm milk
- 1 packet (2 ¼ tsp) dry yeast
- ¼ cup sugar
- 1 egg
- 3 tablespoons butter, melted
- ½ teaspoon salt
- ¾ cup poppy seed filling (store-bought or homemade)
- Egg wash (1 egg yolk + 1 tbsp milk)

## Instructions

1. In a bowl, combine warm milk, sugar, and yeast. Let sit 10 minutes until foamy.
2. Add flour, egg, melted butter, and salt. Knead until smooth. Let rise 1 hour.
3. Divide dough into small balls. Flatten and fill each with a spoonful of poppy filling. Pinch to seal.
4. Place seam-side down on baking tray. Brush with egg wash.
5. Bake at 375°F (190°C) for 20-25 minutes until golden.

**Notes:**
- Storage: Store in an airtight container for up to 3 days. Freeze for up to 2 months.

# CHLEB ORZECHOWY

Nut Bread adds a festive crunch to the holiday table. Walnuts, often used in Polish Christmas baking, symbolize wisdom and strength—making this loaf both delicious and meaningful.

PREP TIME: 2 - 2.5 HRS
COOK TIME: 35 - 45 MIN
SERVINGS: 12 SLICES

## Ingredients

- 2 cups all-purpose flour
- ½ cup whole wheat flour
- 2 teaspoons baking powder
- ½ teaspoon salt
- 1 cup chopped walnuts or mixed nuts
- 1 egg
- 1 cup buttermilk or kefir
- ¼ cup honey or brown sugar
- 2 tablespoons melted butter

## Instructions

1. Preheat oven to 350°F (175°C). Grease a loaf pan.
2. In a bowl, mix flours, baking powder, salt, and nuts.
3. In another bowl, beat egg with buttermilk, honey, and butter.
4. Combine wet and dry ingredients. Pour into loaf pan.
5. Bake 45-55 minutes until toothpick comes out clean.

**Notes:**
- Storage: Store in an airtight container for up to 3 days. Freeze for up to 3 months.

# CHLEB Z SUSZONYMI ŚLIWKAMI

This subtly sweet Prune Bread features dried plums, a nod to Polish orchard traditions. Prunes bring richness and moisture to the loaf and are thought to aid digestion after the big Christmas Eve feast!

 **PREP TIME** 2 - 2.5 HRS   **COOK TIME** 35 - 45 MIN   **SERVINGS** 12 SLICES

## Ingredients

- 2 cups all-purpose flour
- 1 teaspoon baking soda
- ½ teaspoon salt
- 1 teaspoon cinnamon
- ½ teaspoon nutmeg
- 1 cup chopped dried prunes
- ½ cup chopped walnuts (optional)
- 2 eggs
- ½ cup sugar
- ½ cup oil
- 1 cup buttermilk or sour cream

## Instructions

1. Preheat oven to 350°F (175°C). Grease a loaf pan.
2. Mix flour, baking soda, salt, and spices in a bowl.
3. In another bowl, beat eggs with sugar, oil, and buttermilk. Stir in prunes and nuts.
4. Combine mixtures and pour into loaf pan.
5. Bake 55-60 minutes until done.

**Notes:**

- Storage: Store in an airtight container for up to 3 days. Freeze for up to 3 months.

# CHLEBEK MIODOWY

Honey Bread is gently spiced and naturally sweet, echoing the ancient Slavic use of honey as a sacred food. It's often enjoyed with tea or warm milk during quiet holiday evenings.

 **PREP TIME** 2 - 2.5 HRS    **COOK TIME** 35 - 40    **SERVINGS** 12 SLICES

## Ingredients

- 2 ½ cups flour
- 1 teaspoon baking powder
- 1 teaspoon baking soda
- ½ teaspoon cinnamon
- ½ teaspoon cloves
- ½ teaspoon ginger
- 2 eggs
- ¾ cup honey
- ½ cup brown sugar
- ½ cup strong brewed tea or coffee
- ¼ cup oil or melted butter

## Instructions

1. Preheat oven to 350°F (175°C). Grease and flour a loaf pan.
2. In a bowl, mix dry ingredients (flour, baking powder, soda, and spices).
3. In another bowl, beat eggs, honey, sugar, tea, and oil.
4. Combine wet and dry ingredients. Pour into prepared pan.
5. Bake for 45-55 minutes until a toothpick comes out clean.

**Notes:**
- Storage: Store in an airtight container for up to 3 days. Freeze for up to 3 months.

CHAPTER SIX

# Cold & Warm Sides / Salads

# SAŁATKA JARZYNOWA

This colorful Potato-Based Vegetable Salad is a holiday essential in nearly every Polish home. Though recipes vary slightly by family, it always includes mayo, peas, carrots, and love—it's often made the night before so the flavors meld by Christmas Day.

 **PREP TIME** 45 - 60 MIN     **COOK TIME** 20 - 30 MIN     **SERVINGS** 8 - 10

## Ingredients

- 3 medium carrots, peeled
- 2 medium potatoes, peeled
- 1 parsnip (optional)
- 1 cup green peas (frozen or canned)
- 4 dill pickles, finely chopped
- 4 hard-boiled eggs, peeled and chopped
- ½ small onion, finely minced (optional)
- ¾ cup mayonnaise
- 1 teaspoon mustard (optional)
- Salt and pepper to taste

## Instructions

1. Boil carrots, potatoes, and parsnip until fork-tender. Cool, peel if needed, and dice finely.
2. Mix with peas, chopped pickles, eggs, and onion.
3. Stir in mayonnaise and mustard. Season with salt and pepper.
4. Chill at least 2 hours before serving.

**Notes:**
- Storage: Store in an airtight container for up to 3 days.

# SAŁATKA ŚLEDZIOWA WARSTWOWA

Known for its beautiful layers, this salad blends herring, beets, potatoes, and mayo. It's both a visual and flavorful centerpiece on the holiday table and reflects the Eastern European love for combining fish with root vegetables in festive dishes.

 **PREP TIME** 30 - 40 MIN   **COOK TIME** 10 - 15 MIN   **SERVINGS** 6 - 8

## Ingredients

- 4 herring fillets (soaked and chopped)
- 2 medium potatoes, cooked and diced
- 2 carrots, cooked and diced
- 1 small beet, cooked and grated
- 2 hard-boiled eggs, chopped
- ½ cup mayonnaise
- Salt and pepper to taste

## Instructions

1. In a glass bowl, layer in order: herring, potatoes, carrots, eggs, beets.
2. Spread a thin layer of mayonnaise over each layer.
3. Repeat layers if desired. Cover and refrigerate 2+ hours.

**Notes:**

- Storage: Store in an airtight container for up to 3 days.

# BURACZKI Z CHRZANEM

**Sweet beets meet spicy horseradish in this zingy side dish. Traditionally served cold, it's meant to awaken the palate and symbolize vitality, thanks to the beet's bold red color and the horseradish's fiery bite.**

 PREP TIME **15 MIN**    COOK TIME **30 - 40 MIN**    SERVINGS **4 - 6**

## Ingredients

- 3 medium beets, boiled or roasted and peeled
- 2-3 tablespoons grated horseradish (fresh or jarred)
- 1 tablespoon vinegar or lemon juice
- 1 teaspoon sugar
- Salt to taste

## Instructions

1. Grate cooked beets coarsely.
2. Mix with horseradish, vinegar, sugar, and salt. Adjust seasoning.
3. Chill at least 30 minutes before serving.

**Notes:**
- Storage: Store in an airtight container for up to 3 - 4 days. Freeze in a sealed container for up to 2 months.

# KISZONE OGÓRKI

**Polish pickles are naturally fermented, not vinegar-based, giving them a tangy crunch full of probiotics. Often homemade in large jars, they add zing and tradition to any holiday spread—especially when served alongside rich or creamy dishes.**

 PREP TIME **20 MIN**    FERMENT TIME **5 - 10 DAYS**    SERVINGS **1 LITER**

## Ingredients

- 4-6 small cucumbers (Kirby or pickling type)
- 2 garlic cloves
- 1 dill stem with seeds or fresh dill heads
- 2 cups water
- 1 tablespoon salt

## Instructions

1. Dissolve salt in water to create brine.
2. Place cucumbers, garlic, and dill in a clean jar. Pour brine to cover.
3. Cover the jar loosely. Leave at room temperature for 3-5 days.

**Notes:**
- Storage: Store in an airtight container for up to 2 months. Freezing is not recommended.

Chapter Seven

# Christmas Desserts (Desery Bożonarodzeniowe)

# MAKOWIEC

**Makowiec is a symbol of prosperity and fertility in Polish folklore. The rich poppy seed filling is believed to bring luck—so the more poppy seeds you eat at Christmas, the better your new year!**

 PREP TIME
2.5 - 3 HRS

 COOKING TIME
40 - 50 MIN

 SERVINGS
12 SLICES

## Ingredients

- 2 cups all-purpose flour
- 1/3 cup sugar
- 2 ¼ tsp dry yeast
- ½ cup warm milk
- 2 eggs
- ¼ cup butter, melted
- Pinch of salt
- 1 ½ cups poppy seed filling (store-bought or homemade)

## Instructions

1. Combine yeast with warm milk and sugar. Let it sit 10 minutes.
2. Mix flour, eggs, melted butter, salt, and yeast mixture. Knead until smooth. Let rise for 1 hour.
3. Roll the dough into a rectangle. Spread the poppy seed filling evenly.
4. Roll tightly into a log. Let rise for 30 minutes.
5. Bake at 350°F (175°C) for 35-40 minutes.

**Notes:**

- Storage: Store in an airtight container for up to 5 days. Freeze for up to 2 months wrapped in plastic wrap and foil.

# SERNIK

Polish cheesecake, often made with twaróg (curd cheese), is a holiday must-have. Unlike American cheesecake, it's lighter and less sweet—sometimes topped with chocolate or raisins for festive flair.

 **PREP TIME** 30 - 40 MIN   **COOKING TIME** 60 - 70 MIN   **SERVINGS** 12 SLICES

## Ingredients

- 2 pounds twaróg or farmer's cheese
- 1 cup sugar
- 4 eggs
- 1 tsp vanilla
- Zest of 1 lemon
- ¼ cup flour or cornstarch
- ½ cup sour cream

## Instructions

1. Blend cheese until smooth. Add sugar, eggs, vanilla, lemon zest, flour, and sour cream.
2. Pour into a greased springform pan.
3. Bake at 325°F (160°C) for 60-75 minutes.
4. Cool completely, then refrigerate.

**Notes:**

- Storage: Store in an airtight container for up to 5 days. Freeze for up to 2 months wrapped in plastic wrap and foil.

# PIERNIK STAROPOLSKI

This gingerbread is made weeks in advance and aged to deepen its flavor. Spiced and sometimes layered with plum jam, it was once reserved for special occasions—and the longer it aged, the more treasured it became.

 **PREP TIME** 30 MIN     **COOKING TIME** 45 - 60 MIN     **SERVINGS** 12 - 16 SLICES

## Ingredients

- 3 cups flour
- ¾ cup honey
- ¾ cup sugar
- 1 egg
- 1 tsp baking soda
- 1 tsp each: cinnamon, cloves, ginger
- ½ cup milk
- ½ cup butter

## Instructions

1. Warm honey, sugar, butter. Cool slightly. Stir in milk and egg.
2. Mix with flour, spices, and baking soda. Chill dough 2-7 days.
3. Roll and bake at 350°F (175°C) for 15-20 minutes.

**Notes:**

- Storage: Store in an airtight container at room temperature for up to 2 weeks. Freeze for up to 3 months wrapped in plastic wrap and foil.

# PIERNICZKI

**These spiced cookies are fun to decorate and often hung on Christmas trees. Their heart or star shapes make them festive keepsakes, and their warm cinnamon-clove flavor fills homes with nostalgic holiday cheer.**

 PREP TIME **30 MIN**  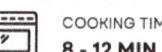 COOKING TIME **8 - 12 MIN**   SERVINGS **40 - 50**

## Ingredients

- 2 cups flour
- ½ cup honey
- ¼ cup sugar
- 1 egg
- 1 tsp baking soda
- 1 tsp gingerbread spice blend

## Instructions

1. Mix ingredients, knead dough, chill 1 hour.
2. Roll, cut shapes, and bake at 350°F (175°C) for 8-10 minutes.

**Notes:**

- Storage: Store in an airtight container at room temperature for up to 3 weeks. Freeze for up to 3 months wrapped in plastic wrap and foil.

# KUTIA

Kutia is rooted in ancient Slavic tradition and often the first dish served at Wigilia. Each spoonful contains wheat for abundance, honey for sweetness, and poppy seeds for luck—making it both symbolic and delicious.

 **PREP TIME** 20 MIN   **COOKING TIME** 1 - 1.5 HRS  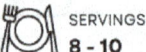 **SERVINGS** 8 - 10

## Ingredients

- 1 cup wheat berries
- ½ cup poppy seeds
- ½ cup chopped nuts
- ½ cup raisins
- ¼ cup honey

## Instructions

1. Soak wheat overnight. Cook until tender. Drain.
2. Soak poppy seeds in hot water, drain, and grind.
3. Mix wheat, poppy seeds, nuts, raisins, and honey.

**Notes:**
- Storage: Store in an airtight container in the refrigerator for up to 3 weeks. Freeze for up to 2 months.

# KLUSKI Z MAKIEM

This sweet noodle dish is traditionally served after Wigilia to welcome blessings and dreams. It's simple, comforting, and filled with poppy seeds—symbols of prosperity in Polish culture.

 **PREP TIME** 20 MIN     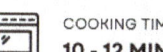 **COOKING TIME** 10 - 12 MIN      **SERVINGS** 6 - 8

## Ingredients

- 8 oz egg noodles
- ½ cup ground poppy seeds
- ¼ cup honey
- ¼ cup chopped nuts or dried fruit

## Instructions

1. Cook noodles, then drain.
2. Mix with poppy seeds, honey, fruit, and nuts

**Notes:**

- Storage: Store in an airtight container in the refrigerator for up to 3 days. Freezing is not recommended.

# ŁAMAŃCE Z MAKIEM

A rustic variation of poppy seed noodles, this dish uses handmade flat dough sheets broken into pieces. It's often sweetened with honey and served with dried fruit or nuts as a symbol of abundance.

 PREP TIME
20 - 30 MIN

 COOKING TIME
NONE

 SERVINGS
6 - 8

## Ingredients

- 1 sheet of flat unleavened dough or pasta
- ½ cup ground poppy seeds
- ¼ cup chopped nuts
- ¼ cup honey

## Instructions

1. Break the dough into pieces, and cook if necessary.
2. Combine with warm honey, poppy seeds, and nuts.

**Notes:**
- Storage: Store in an airtight container in the refrigerator for up to 3 days. Freezing is not recommended.

# KEKS BAKALIOWY

Packed with dried fruit and nuts, this Polish fruitcake is dense, festive, and full of texture. Unlike its infamous Western cousin, Polish keks is beloved—and often baked in long loaves and sliced thin.

 **PREP TIME** 25 - 30 MIN   **COOKING TIME** 50 - 60 MIN   **SERVINGS** 10 - 12 SLICES

## Ingredients

- 1 ½ cups flour
- ½ cup butter
- ½ cup sugar
- 3 eggs
- 1 tsp baking powder
- 1 cup dried fruit and nuts

## Instructions

1. Cream butter, sugar, and eggs. Add flour, baking powder, fruit, and nuts.
2. Pour into pan, bake at 350°F (175°C) for 40-50 minutes.

**Notes:**

- Storage: Store in an airtight container at room temperature for up to 5 days. Freeze for up to 3 months wrapped in plastic wrap and foil.

# JABŁECZNIK

**This cozy apple dessert features layers of tart apples between delicate cake or shortcrust. It's Poland's answer to apple pie—served warm or cold and always a crowd-pleaser, especially at Christmas gatherings.**

 **PREP TIME** 30 MIN     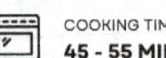 **COOKING TIME** 45 - 55 MIN      **SERVINGS** 12 SLICES

## Ingredients

- 2 cups flour
- ½ cup sugar
- ½ cup butter
- 2 eggs
- 4 apples, peeled and sliced
- 1 tsp cinnamon

## Instructions

1. Mix the dough. Press half into the pan.
2. Layer apples with cinnamon and sugar. Top with the remaining dough.
3. Bake at 350°F (175°C) for 45 minutes.

**Notes:**

- Storage: Store covered at room temperature or in the refrigerator for 2 to 5 days. Freeze for up to 3 months wrapped in plastic wrap and foil.

# TORT ORZECHOWY

**Nutty, rich, and often layered with cream, this cake was once considered a luxury. Walnuts symbolize wisdom and strength, making this a meaningful dessert for family celebrations and holiday feasts.**

 **PREP TIME** 40 - 60 MIN    **COOKING TIME** 30 - 40 MIN    **SERVINGS** 12 SLICES

## Ingredients

- 6 eggs
- 1 cup ground walnuts
- ½ cup sugar
- ¼ cup flour
- 1 tsp vanilla

## Instructions

1. Beat yolks with sugar. Fold in walnuts, flour, and beaten egg whites.
2. Bake at 350°F (175°C) for 30-35 minutes.

**Notes:**

- Storage: Store covered in the refrigerator for 4 to 5 days. Freeze for up to 2 months wrapped in plastic wrap and foil.

# RACUCHY Z JABŁKAMI

Soft and fluffy with warm apple chunks inside, racuchy are like Polish pancakes. Traditionally fried on Christmas morning, they bring joy to kids and adults alike—especially when dusted with powdered sugar.

 **PREP TIME** 15 - 20 MIN     **COOKING TIME** 15 - 20 MIN     **SERVINGS** 4 - 6

## Ingredients

- 1 cup flour
- 1 egg
- ½ cup milk
- 1 apple, grated or sliced
- 1 tsp baking powder
- Pinch of salt
- Oil for frying

## Instructions

1. Mix batter. Fold in apples.
2. Fry spoonfuls in hot oil until golden.

**Notes:**
- Storage: Store in an airtight container in the refrigerator for 2 to 3 days. Freeze for up to 2 months.

# KULEBIAK Z MAKIEM

This festive rolled pastry is like a larger cousin of makowiec, often braided or beautifully shaped. Stuffed with spiced poppy seed filling, it's a showstopper dessert that doubles as a centerpiece.

**PREP TIME** 30 - 40 MINS  
**COOKING TIME** 35 - 45 MIN  
**SERVINGS** 8 - 10 SLICES

## Ingredients

- 2 cups all-purpose flour
- 1/3 cup sugar
- 2 ¼ tsp dry yeast
- ½ cup warm milk
- 2 eggs
- ¼ cup butter, melted
- Pinch of salt
- 1 ½ cups poppy seed filling (store-bought or homemade)

## Instructions

1. Roll dough, fill with poppy mixture.
2. Shape into a log or braid. Let rise.
3. Bake at 350°F (175°C) until golden.

**Notes:**
- Storage: Store in an airtight container in the refrigerator for up to 5 days. Freeze for up to 2 months wrapped in plastic wrap and foil.

# STRUCLA Z SEREM

Strucla is a yeasted roll filled with sweet cheese, often twaróg. Baked to golden perfection and dusted with sugar, it's a comforting blend of tangy and sweet—perfect with a cup of tea.

**PREP TIME:** 30 - 40 MINS
**COOKING TIME:** 30 - 40 MIN
**SERVINGS:** 8 - 10 SLICES

## Ingredients

- 2 cups flour
- ½ cup butter
- 2 egg yolks
- ½ cup sour cream
- Filling: 1 cup farmer's cheese, ¼ cup sugar, 1 egg yolk, vanilla

## Instructions

1. Mix dough, chill. Roll out and fill with cheese.
2. Roll into a log. Bake at 350°F (175°C) for 35-40 minutes.

**Notes:**

- Storage: Store in an airtight container in the refrigerator for up to 5 days. Freeze for up to 2 months wrapped in plastic wrap and foil.

# SZARLOTKA Z KRUSZONKĄ

Szarlotka features layers of cinnamon apples under a buttery crumb topping. It's not overly sweet, making it a favorite for both dessert and breakfast. Served warm, it's pure holiday comfort.

 **PREP TIME** 30 - 40 MINS   **COOKING TIME** 45 - 55 MIN   **SERVINGS** 12 PIECES

## Ingredients

- 2 cups flour
- ¾ cup butter
- ½ cup sugar
- 5 apples, sliced
- 1 tsp cinnamon

## Instructions

1. Press 2/3 of the dough into the pan. Layer apples with cinnamon and sugar.
2. Crumble the remaining dough on top.
3. Bake at 375°F (190°C) for 40–45 minutes.

**Notes:**

- Storage: Store covered at room temperature for 1 to 2 days. Store in an airtight container in the refrigerator for up to 5 days. Freeze for up to 2 months wrapped in plastic wrap and foil.

# BABKA MIGDAŁOWA

This elegant bundt cake, flavored with ground almonds, is soft, fragrant, and slightly sweet. Often served with a dusting of powdered sugar, it's a light yet festive treat after a rich Wigilia meal.

**PREP TIME** 20 - 25 MIN
**COOKING TIME** 45 - 55 MIN
**SERVINGS** 12 SLICES

## Ingredients

- 1 cup butter
- 1 cup sugar
- 4 eggs
- 1 ½ cups flour
- 1 tsp baking powder
- 1 tsp almond extract
- ½ cup ground almonds

## Instructions

1. Cream butter, sugar, and eggs. Add dry ingredients and extract.
2. Bake in a greased bundt pan at 350°F (175°C) for 40-45 minutes.

**Notes:**
- Storage: Store covered at room temperature for 3 days. Store in an airtight container in the refrigerator for up to 5 days. Freeze for up to 3 months wrapped in plastic wrap and foil.

# MAZUREK ORZECHOWY

**Mazurek is a traditional Polish Easter dessert, known for its rich toppings and decorative flair—often resembling a piece of edible art!**

 PREP TIME 25 - 30 MIN   COOKING TIME 20 - 25 MIN   SERVINGS 12 SLICES

## Ingredients

- 1 ½ cups flour
- ½ cup butter
- ¼ cup sugar
- 1 egg
- 1 cup chopped nuts
- ½ cup honey or jam

## Instructions

1. Mix dough, chill. Press into tart pan.
2. Spread honey or jam, top with nuts.
3. Bake at 350°F (175°C) for 25-30 minutes.

**Notes:**

- Storage: Store covered at room temperature for up to 5 days. Freezing is not recommended.

Chapter Eight

# Christmas Drinks

# KOMPOT Z SUSZU

This traditional Polish dried fruit punch isn't just tasty —it's also a holiday superstition! Drinking Kompot z Suszu on Christmas Eve is said to bring health and good luck for the whole year. So every sip is like a little festive magic!

 PREP TIME **5 MIN**   COOK TIME **30 - 40 MIN**   SERVINGS **6 - 8**

## Ingredients

- 1 cup dried prunes
- 1 cup dried apples or pears
- ½ cup dried apricots (optional)
- 6 cups of water
- 2-3 tablespoons honey or sugar
- 2 cloves
- 1 cinnamon stick
- 1 strip of lemon zest (optional)

## Instructions

1. Rinse dried fruit and place in a pot with water, spices, and zest.
2. Bring to boil, reduce to a simmer for 30-40 minutes.
3. Sweeten with honey or sugar to taste. Chill or serve warm.

**Notes:**

- Storage: Store in an airtight container for up to 5 days. Freeze in a sealed container for up to 2 months.

# KOMPOT Z SUSZONYCH ŚLIWEK

In Poland, dried plum kompot isn't just a tasty drink—it's also known as a natural digestive aid, especially during holiday feasts! The sweet and slightly smoky flavor makes it a nostalgic favorite.

 **PREP TIME** 5 - 10 MIN    **COOKING TIME** 25 - 30 MIN    **SERVINGS** 4 - 6

## Ingredients

- 2 cups dried prunes
- 4 cups water
- 1 tablespoon sugar (optional)
- 1 cinnamon stick
- Juice of ½ lemon (optional)

## Instructions

1. Rinse prunes and place in pot with water and cinnamon.
2. Simmer for 30 minutes until soft. Add sugar and lemon juice if desired.

**Notes:**

- Storage: Store in a glass jar in the refrigerator for up to 5 days. Freeze in freezer-safe containers for up to 3 months.

# MIÓD PITNY

**Miód pitny is one of Poland's oldest traditional drinks, dating back to medieval times. It was once considered more precious than wine and often reserved for royalty and special occasions!**

PREP TIME: 30 MIN  |  COOKING TIME: 30 - 60 MIN  |  SERVINGS: 4 - 6

## Ingredients

- 1 cup honey
- 3 cups water
- 1 cinnamon stick
- 2 cloves
- 2-3 allspice berries
- Optional: splash of vodka or wine for warmth

## Instructions

1. In a pot, dissolve the honey in water. Add spices.
2. Simmer gently for 15 minutes. Strain.
3. Add alcohol if using. Serve warm.

**Notes:**
- Storage: Store in sterilized bottles in a cool, dark place for up to 6 months. Once opened, store in the fridge and consume within 1 - 2 months. Freezing is not recommended.

# GRZANIEC Z PRZYPRAWAMI

Grzaniec has been enjoyed in Poland for centuries, especially during Christmas markets and winter festivals. Each family or region may have its own spice blend, making every cup a little different!

 **PREP TIME** 5 - 10 MIN   **COOKING TIME** 10 - 15 MIN   **SERVINGS** 4 - 6

## Ingredients

- 1 bottle dry red wine
- ¼ cup sugar or honey
- 1 cinnamon stick
- 3 cloves
- 2-3 strips of orange peel
- 2 whole allspice berries
- Optional: shot of rum or brandy

## Instructions

1. In a saucepan, combine wine, sugar, and spices.
2. Heat gently—do not boil—until warm and aromatic.
3. Strain and serve.

**Notes:**

- Storage: Store in a sealed jar in the refrigerator for up to 3 days. Freezing is not recommended.

# HERBATA Z KONFITURĄ

Drinking tea with jam was a popular tradition in Eastern Europe, especially in Russia and Poland, where people would stir fruit preserves like raspberry or blackcurrant into their tea for sweetness and flavor instead of using sugar!

 **PREP TIME** 5 MIN   **COOKING TIME** NONE   **SERVINGS** 1

## Ingredients

- 1 bag of black tea or loose leaf
- 1 teaspoon raspberry or cherry preserves per cup
- Boiling water
- Optional: lemon slice

## Instructions

1. Brew tea to the desired strength.
2. Stir in fruit preserves until dissolved.
3. Add lemon if using.

**Notes:**

- Storage: Store in the refrigerator for 1 day. Freezing is not recommended.

# NAPAR Z GOŹDZIKÓW I POMARAŃCZY

**Clove and orange infusions have been used for centuries to support the immune system and warm the body in cold seasons. The scent is also known to be naturally calming and festive—perfect for winter evenings!**

 **PREP TIME** 5 MIN   COOKING TIME 10 - 15 MIN   SERVINGS 4 CUPS

## Ingredients

- 2 cups water
- 6 whole cloves
- Peel of 1 orange (or slices)
- 1-2 tablespoons honey
- Optional: small cinnamon stick

## Instructions

1. Bring water, cloves, and orange peel to a gentle boil.
2. Simmer 10-15 minutes. Strain.
3. Stir in honey to taste.

**Notes:**

- Storage: Store in the refrigerator in a sealed jar for 2 to 3 days. Freezing is not recommended.

# Chapter Nine
# Vegetarian Holiday Mains

# KLOPS Z WARZYW I ORZECHÓW

Klops z Warzyw i Orzechów became especially popular in vegetarian Polish households as a meat-free holiday alternative. Packed with protein and flavor, it often surprises meat-lovers with its hearty texture!

 **PREP TIME** 20 - 30 MIN
 **COOKING TIME** 45 - 60 MIN
 **SERVINGS** 6 - 8

## Ingredients

- 1 cup cooked lentils or beans
- 1 cup breadcrumbs
- 1 cup mixed vegetables (carrots, celery, onion), finely chopped
- ½ cup chopped walnuts
- 2 eggs
- 2 tablespoons oil
- 1 teaspoon marjoram
- Salt and pepper to taste

## Instructions

1. Preheat oven to 375°F (190°C). Grease a loaf pan or oven dish.
2. Sauté chopped vegetables until soft. Mix with lentils, breadcrumbs, nuts, eggs, and seasoning.
3. Press into the loaf pan or roll into balls. Bake 40-50 minutes until firm and golden.

**Notes:**

- Storage: Store in an airtight container in the refrigerator for up to 5 days. Freeze for up to 2 months wrapped in plastic wrap or foil.

# PASZTET Z SOCZEWICY

Pasztet z soczewicy is a favorite meatless twist on traditional Polish pâté, often served during Wigilia (Christmas Eve) when no meat is eaten. It's rich in plant protein and can be made with a mix of herbs, mushrooms, or veggies for extra flavor!

 **PREP TIME** 20 - 30 MIN   **COOKING TIME** 45 - 50 MIN   **SERVINGS** 6 - 8

## Ingredients

- 1 cup green or brown lentils, cooked
- 1 small onion, chopped
- 1 carrot, grated
- 1 tablespoon oil
- ½ cup breadcrumbs
- 1 egg (or flax egg)
- Salt, pepper, and marjoram to taste

## Instructions

1. Sauté onion and carrot in oil until soft.
2. Blend lentils, sautéed vegetables, egg, and seasoning until smooth.
3. Mix in breadcrumbs. Press into a small loaf pan. Bake at 375°F (190°C) for 30–35 minutes.

**Notes:**

- Storage: Store in an airtight container in the refrigerator for up to 5 days. Freeze for up to 2 months wrapped in plastic wrap or foil.

# NALEŚNIKI Z KAPUSTĄ I GRZYBAMI

Naleśniki z kapustą i grzybami are a beloved Christmas Eve dish in Poland. They are often breaded and fried into crispy croquettes (called krokiety) and served with a warm bowl of barszcz czerwony (beet soup).

 **PREP TIME** 30 - 40 MIN  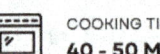 **COOKING TIME** 40 - 50 MIN   **SERVINGS** 4 - 5

## Ingredients

**Crepe Batter:**
- 1 cup flour
- 1 cup milk
- 1 egg
- 1 tablespoon oil
- Pinch of salt

**Filling:**
- 2 cups sauerkraut, rinsed and chopped
- 1 cup mushrooms, chopped
- 1 onion, chopped
- Salt and pepper to taste

## Instructions

1. Mix crepe batter, let rest 20 minutes. Cook thin crepes.
2. Sauté the onion and mushrooms. Add sauerkraut, cook 15 minutes.
3. Fill crepes and roll.

**Notes:**
- Storage: Store in the fridge in an airtight container for up to 4 days. Freeze for up to 2 months wrapped in parchment.

# KROKIETY Z KAPUSTĄ I GRZYBAMI

**Krokiety are a traditional Polish festive dish, especially popular during Christmas Eve dinner, often served with hot barszcz czerwony (beet soup) for dipping!**

 PREP TIME: 45 - 60 MIN   COOKING TIME: 20 - 25 MIN   SERVINGS: 4

## Ingredients

**Filling:**
- 2 cups sauerkraut, rinsed and chopped
- 1 cup mushrooms, chopped
- 1 onion, chopped
- Salt and pepper to taste

**Additional Ingredients:**
- Flour, breadcrumbs, and eggs for breading

## Instructions

1. Fill crepes and roll tightly.
2. Dip in flour, beaten egg, then breadcrumbs.
3. Fry in oil until golden and crispy.

**Notes:**
- Storage: Store in the fridge in an airtight container for up to 3 days. Freeze for up to 2 months individually wrapped in plastic wrap.

# PLACKI ZIEMNIACZANE Z GRZYBAMI

**Placki ziemniaczane are so popular in Poland they even have a National Potato Pancake Day celebrated every year! They are a beloved comfort food and often served with sour cream or mushroom sauce.**

 PREP TIME **30 MIN**    COOKING TIME **20 - 25 MIN**    SERVINGS **3 - 4**

## Ingredients

- 4 potatoes, grated
- 1 onion, grated
- 1 egg
- 2 tablespoons flour
- Salt and pepper
- Oil for frying
- Optional: sautéed mushrooms or mushroom sauce

## Instructions

1. Grate and drain excess liquid from potatoes. Mix with onion, egg, flour, salt, and pepper.
2. Fry spoonfuls in oil until golden on both sides.
3. Top with sautéed mushrooms or serve with mushroom sauce.

**Notes:**

- Storage: Store in the fridge in an airtight container for up to 2 days. Freeze for up to 2 months individually wrapped in plastic wrap.

# PASZTECIKI Z GRZYBAMI

**Paszteciki are a traditional Polish snack often enjoyed during holidays and special occasions, and they pair perfectly with barszcz (beet soup) for a classic Polish combo!**

 **PREP TIME** 40 MIN     **COOKING TIME** 25 - 30 MIN     **SERVINGS** 4

## Ingredients

- 1 sheet puff pastry (or yeast dough)
- 1 cup mushrooms, finely chopped
- 1 onion, chopped
- Salt and pepper to taste

## Instructions

1. Sauté the onion and mushrooms until soft. Season.
2. Cut pastry into squares. Add filling, fold into triangles or rolls.
3. Brush with egg wash. Bake at 375°F (190°C) until golden.

**Notes:**

- Storage: Store in the fridge in an airtight container for up to 3 days. Freeze for up to 2 months.

# PIECZONE PIEROGI Z KAPUSTĄ

**Baked pierogi are a delicious twist on the traditional boiled version, offering a crispy outside and tender inside — perfect for a comforting, hearty meal!**

 PREP TIME **20 MIN**   COOKING TIME **25 - 30 MIN**   SERVINGS **4 - 5**

## Ingredients

- Pierogi dough (as per traditional recipe)
- Filling: 2 cups sauerkraut, 1 cup mushrooms, 1 onion, sautéed and seasoned
- Egg wash

## Instructions

1. Fill pierogi dough with sauerkraut mixture. Fold and seal.
2. Brush with egg wash. Bake at 375°F (190°C) for 20-25 minutes.

**Notes:**
- Storage: Store in the fridge in an airtight container for up to 2 days. Freeze uncooked pierogi on a tray for up to 2 months.

# KASZA GRYCZANA Z GRZYBAMI

**Buckwheat (kasza gryczana) is naturally gluten-free and packed with nutrients, making it a healthy and traditional staple in Polish cuisine!**

 PREP TIME
**10 MIN**

 COOKING TIME
**30 MIN**

 SERVINGS
**4**

## Ingredients

- 1 cup roasted buckwheat groats
- 2 cups water or vegetable broth
- 1 cup wild mushrooms, chopped
- 1 onion, chopped
- 2 tablespoons oil or butter
- Salt and pepper

## Instructions

1. Cook buckwheat in water or broth until fluffy.
2. Sauté the onion and mushrooms. Mix with cooked buckwheat. Season.

**Notes:**
- Storage: Store in the fridge in an airtight container for up to 3 days. Freeze for up to 2 months.

## Chapter Ten
# Christmas Cookies (Ciasteczka Świąteczne)

# CIASTECZKA KORZENNE

Ciasteczka Korzenne are often enjoyed during the holiday season in Poland, filled with warm spices like cinnamon, cloves, and ginger — a perfect cozy treat!

 **PREP TIME** 20 MIN     **COOKING TIME** 10 - 12 MIN     **SERVINGS** 30 COOKIES

## Ingredients

- 2 ½ cups flour
- ¾ cup brown sugar
- 1 tsp baking soda
- 1 tsp cinnamon
- ½ tsp each: ground ginger, nutmeg, cloves
- 1 egg
- ½ cup butter
- ¼ cup honey or molasses

## Instructions

1. Mix dry ingredients in a bowl.
2. In a separate bowl, beat butter, sugar, egg, and honey. Combine with dry ingredients.
3. Chill the dough for 1 hour. Roll, cut shapes, and bake at 350°F (175°C) for 8-10 minutes.

**Notes:**
- Storage: Store in an airtight container at room temperature for up to 1 week. Freeze in a sealed container or freezer bag for up to 3 months.

# CIASTECZKA MIGDAŁOWE

Almond cookies have been a beloved treat in Polish kitchens for centuries, often enjoyed with a cup of tea or coffee, and are known for their delicate nutty flavor and crisp texture!

 **PREP TIME** 15 MIN
 **COOKING TIME** 12 - 15 MIN
 **SERVINGS** 25 - 30 COOKIES

## Ingredients

- 1 cup ground almonds
- 1 cup flour
- ½ cup butter
- ½ cup sugar
- 1 egg
- ½ tsp almond extract

## Instructions

1. Cream butter and sugar. Add egg and extract. Mix in almonds and flour.
2. Form small balls or crescents. Bake at 350°F (175°C) for 10-12 minutes

**Notes:**

- Storage: Store in an airtight container at room temperature for up to 1 week. Freeze in a sealed container or freezer bag for up to 3 months.

# CIASTECZKA KOKOSOWE

Coconut cookies became especially popular in Poland during the 20th century when coconut flakes became more widely available, giving a tropical twist to traditional Polish baking!

 **PREP TIME** 15 MIN

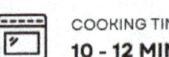 **COOKING TIME** 10 - 12 MIN

 **SERVINGS** 20 - 25 COOKIES

## Ingredients

- 2 cups shredded coconut
- 2 egg whites
- ½ cup sugar
- ½ tsp vanilla extract

## Instructions

1. Beat egg whites until frothy. Add sugar, coconut, and vanilla.
2. Drop spoonfuls onto parchment. Bake at 325°F (160°C) for 12-15 minutes.

**Notes:**
- Storage: Store in an airtight container at room temperature for up to 1 week. Freeze in a sealed container or freezer bag for up to 3 months.

# KRUCHE CIASTECZKA Z MARMOLADĄ

These cookies are often made in Poland for Christmas and Easter, and traditionally filled with rose petal marmalade—a beloved old-world flavor still used today!

 **PREP TIME** 20 MIN   **COOKING TIME** 12 - 15 MIN   **SERVINGS** 20 - 25 COOKIES

## Ingredients

- 1 ½ cups flour
- ½ cup butter
- ¼ cup sugar
- 1 egg yolk
- ½ tsp vanilla
- Fruit marmalade or jam

## Instructions

1. Mix butter, sugar, yolk, and vanilla. Add flour. Chill the dough.
2. Roll into balls, press thumb in center. Fill with jam.
3. Bake at 350°F (175°C) for 12-15 minutes.

**Notes:**

- Storage: Store in an airtight container at room temperature for up to 1 week. Freeze in a sealed container or freezer bag for up to 3 months.

# ANYŻKOWE CIASTECZKA

**Anise cookies have been enjoyed in Poland for centuries and were once believed to help with digestion—so they were often served after big holiday meals!**

 PREP TIME **15 - 20 MIN**   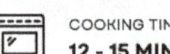 COOKING TIME **12 - 15 MIN**   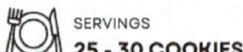 SERVINGS **25 - 30 COOKIES**

## Ingredients

- 2 cups flour
- ½ tsp baking powder
- ½ cup butter
- ½ cup sugar
- 1 egg
- 1 tsp anise extract or seeds

## Instructions

1. Cream butter and sugar. Add egg and anise. Mix in flour.
2. Roll and cut or pipe shapes. Bake at 350°F (175°C) for 10-12 minutes.

**Notes:**
- Storage: Store in an airtight container at room temperature for up to 2 weeks. Freeze in a sealed container or freezer bag for up to 3 months.

# CIASTECZKA CYTRYNOWE

**Lemon cookies are loved for their bright, zesty flavor and are often made during spring and summer—but in Poland, they're also popular on holiday cookie trays for a refreshing contrast to richer treats!**

| | | |
|---|---|---|
| **PREP TIME** <br> 15 - 20 MIN | **COOKING TIME** <br> 10 - 12 MIN | **SERVINGS** <br> 25 - 30 COOKIES |

## Ingredients

- 2 cups flour
- ½ cup sugar
- ½ cup butter
- 1 egg
- Zest of 1 lemon
- 2 tbsp lemon juice
- ½ tsp baking powder

## Instructions

1. Cream butter, sugar, egg, zest, and juice. Mix in flour and baking powder.
2. Roll and cut shapes or slice-and-bake.
3. Bake at 350°F (175°C) for 10-12 minutes.

**Notes:**

- Storage: Store in an airtight container at room temperature for up to 2 weeks. Freeze in a sealed container or freezer bag for up to 3 months.

# CIASTECZKA Z ORZECHAMI LASKOWYMI

Hazelnuts are a classic ingredient in many European desserts. These cookies have a naturally nutty, buttery flavor and are especially popular around Christmas in Poland!

 **PREP TIME** 20 MIN   **COOKING TIME** 12 - 15 MIN   **SERVINGS** 25 - 30 COOKIES

## Ingredients

- 1 cup flour
- ½ cup ground hazelnuts
- ½ cup butter
- ¼ cup sugar
- ½ tsp vanilla

## Instructions

1. Mix all ingredients into a crumbly dough. Chill 30 minutes.
2. Roll into small balls or slice short logs.
3. Bake at 350°F (175°C) for 10-12 minutes.

**Notes:**
- Storage: Store in an airtight container at room temperature for up to 2 weeks. Freeze in a sealed container or freezer bag for up to 3 months.

# CIASTECZKA WANILIOWE

Vanilla cookies are often shaped into crescents or rounds in Poland and are especially popular during the holiday season. The vanilla aroma makes them feel cozy and festive!

**PREP TIME** 15 - 20 MINS  **COOKING TIME** 10 - 12 MIN  **SERVINGS** 25 - 30 COOKIES

## Ingredients

- 1 ½ cups flour
- ¾ cup butter
- ½ cup ground almonds or walnuts
- ¼ cup sugar
- 1 tsp vanilla extract

## Instructions

1. Mix the dough. Shape into crescents. Bake at 350°F (175°C) for 12 minutes.
2. Cool and dust with powdered sugar.

**Notes:**

- Storage: Store in an airtight container at room temperature for up to 2 weeks. Freeze in a sealed container or freezer bag for up to 3 months.

# CIASTECZKA Z PRZYPRAWAMI DO PIERNIKA

These cookies are made with traditional piernik spice mix, which includes cinnamon, cloves, nutmeg, and ginger. They're a staple in Polish Christmas celebrations and often used to decorate holiday tables—or even Christmas trees!

 **PREP TIME** 20 - 30 MINS    **COOKING TIME** 8 - 12 MIN    **SERVINGS** 30 - 40 COOKIES

## Ingredients

- 2 ½ cups flour
- ½ cup sugar
- ½ cup honey or molasses
- ½ cup butter
- 1 egg
- 1 tsp baking soda
- 1 tbsp gingerbread spice mix

## Instructions

1. Mix dry and wet ingredients. Chill the dough.
2. Roll, cut festive shapes. Bake at 350°F (175°C) for 8-10 minutes.

**Notes:**

- Storage: Store in an airtight container at room temperature for up to 2 weeks. Freeze in a sealed container or freezer bag for up to 3 months.

Chapter Eleven

# Extras & Festive Additions

# CHRZAN DOMOWY

**Chrzan Domowy is a bold and spicy Polish condiment made from freshly grated horseradish root. It's a traditional addition to Polish Easter celebrations, often served alongside cold meats, hard-boiled eggs, or white sausage (biała kiełbasa). The fiery flavor symbolizes the strength and freshness of spring and new beginnings in Polish culture.**

 PREP TIME
15 - 20 MIN

 COOKING TIME
NONE

 SERVINGS
1 CUP

## Ingredients

- 1 cup freshly grated horseradish root
- 2 tablespoons white vinegar
- 1 teaspoon sugar
- ½ teaspoon salt
- 1-2 tablespoons water (as needed)

## Instructions

1. Peel and finely grate horseradish root in a well-ventilated area.
2. Mix with vinegar, sugar, salt, and a little water to reach the desired consistency.
3. Store in a sealed jar in the fridge for up to 2 weeks.

**Notes:**
- Storage: Store in a clean, airtight jar in the refrigerator for up to 4 weeks. Freezing is not recommended.

# SOS GRZYBOWY

Sos Grzybowy is a rich and creamy mushroom sauce often made with wild or dried mushrooms. It is a traditional Polish festive dish served especially during Christmas Eve dinner (Wigilia). The sauce symbolizes the abundance of forests in Poland and adds a special earthy flavor to pierogi, kluski, or meat dishes, making holiday meals cozy and memorable.

 **PREP TIME** 15 - 20 MIN    **COOKING TIME** 30 - 40 MIN    **SERVINGS** 4

## Ingredients

- 1 cup dried wild mushrooms, soaked and chopped
- 1 small onion, finely chopped
- 2 tablespoons butter or oil
- 1 tablespoon flour
- 1 ½ cups mushroom soaking liquid or vegetable broth
- ½ cup sour cream (optional)
- Salt and pepper to taste

## Instructions

1. Sauté the onion in butter until soft. Add mushrooms and cook for 5 minutes.
2. Sprinkle flour and stir well. Slowly add broth, stirring constantly.
3. Simmer until thickened. Stir in sour cream off the heat if using. Season to taste.

**Notes:**

- Storage: Store in a clean, airtight jar in the refrigerator for up to 4 days. Freeze in freezer-safe containers for up to 2 months.

# SOS CHRZANOWY Z JABŁKIEM

Sos Chrzanowy z Jabłkiem is a tangy and slightly sweet horseradish sauce with fresh apple bits. It is a popular Polish festive sauce, especially served during Easter and Christmas meals. The sharpness of horseradish combined with the sweetness of apple perfectly complements meats and symbolizes the fresh start of spring and renewal in Polish traditions.

 **PREP TIME** 10 MIN     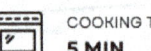 **COOKING TIME** 5 MIN      **SERVINGS** 4

## Ingredients

- 2 tablespoons prepared horseradish
- 1 apple, peeled and grated
- ½ cup sour cream or plain yogurt
- 1 teaspoon sugar
- Pinch of salt

## Instructions

1. Mix all ingredients together until creamy.
2. Chill for 30 minutes to blend flavors.

**Notes:**

- Storage: Store in a clean, airtight jar in the refrigerator for up to 5 days. Freezing is not recommended.

# MASŁO CZOSNKOWE

Masło Czosnkowe is a beloved Polish festive spread often served during holiday meals like Christmas and Easter. Its rich garlic flavor adds a special touch to bread, meats, and grilled dishes, making it a simple but flavorful tradition enjoyed by many Polish families during celebrations.

 **PREP TIME** 10 MIN   **COOKING TIME** NONE   **SERVINGS** 6

## Ingredients

- ½ cup butter, softened
- 2 cloves garlic, minced
- 1 tablespoon chopped parsley or dill
- Salt to taste

## Instructions

1. Mash garlic into softened butter.
2. Stir in herbs and salt. Mix until smooth.
3. Shape into a log and refrigerate until firm.

**Notes:**

- Storage: Store in a clean, airtight container in the refrigerator for up to 1 week. Freeze for up to 3 months in small portions.

# SOS KOPERKOWY

Sos Koperkowy is a classic Polish sauce often served during festive occasions like Christmas and Easter. Made with fresh dill, it pairs perfectly with fish, potatoes, and boiled meats — adding a fresh, herbal flavor that's loved in Polish holiday traditions.

 **PREP TIME** 10 MIN      **COOKING TIME** 10 MIN      **SERVINGS** 4

## Ingredients

- 1 tablespoon butter
- 1 tablespoon flour
- 1 cup milk or cream
- 2 tablespoons fresh dill, chopped
- Salt and pepper to taste

## Instructions

1. Melt butter in a saucepan. Stir in flour to form a roux.
2. Slowly add milk, stirring constantly until thickened.
3. Add dill, season, and cook another minute.

**Notes:**

- Storage: Store in a clean, airtight container in the refrigerator for 3 to 4 days. Freezing is not recommended.

# ZIEMNIAKI Z KOPERKIEM

Ziemniaki z Koperkiem is a simple but beloved Polish side dish often served during festive meals, especially at Christmas and Easter. The fresh dill adds a fragrant, bright touch that complements many traditional Polish dishes, making it a staple on holiday tables.

 **PREP TIME** 10 MIN      **COOKING TIME** 20 MIN      **SERVINGS** 4

## Ingredients

- 2 pounds small potatoes, peeled
- 2 tablespoons butter
- 2 tablespoons chopped fresh dill
- Salt to taste

## Instructions

1. Boil potatoes in salted water until tender. Drain.
2. Toss with butter and dill.

**Notes:**
- Storage: Store in an airtight container in the refrigerator and consume within 2 days. Freezing is not recommended.

# KLUSKI DROŻDŻOWE

Kluski Drożdżowe are a traditional Polish festive dish often served during holidays like Christmas and Easter. These soft, fluffy yeast dumplings are perfect for soaking up rich sauces or gravies, making them a cozy favorite at family gatherings.

 **PREP TIME** 30 MIN    **COOKING TIME** 15 MIN    **SERVINGS** 4

## Ingredients

- 2 cups all-purpose flour
- 1 packet (2¼ tsp) active dry yeast
- ¾ cup warm milk
- 1 tablespoon sugar
- 1 egg
- 2 tablespoons butter, melted
- ¼ teaspoon salt

## Instructions

1. In a bowl, combine yeast, sugar, and warm milk. Let it sit for 10 minutes until foamy.
2. Add flour, egg, butter, and salt. Mix and knead into a soft dough.
3. Cover and let rise in a warm place for about 1 hour.
4. Divide the dough into small balls. Let rise again for 20 minutes.
5. Steam dumplings in a steamer or over boiling water for 10-15 minutes, until puffed and cooked through.

**Notes:**
- Storage: Store in an airtight container in the refrigerator and consume within 2 days. Freeze in a single layer for up to 3 months.

# PYZY ZIEMNIACZANE

Pyzy Ziemniaczane are a beloved Polish festive dish, especially popular during holidays and family celebrations. These hearty potato dumplings can be stuffed or plain and are perfect comfort food during chilly seasons!

 **PREP TIME** 30 MIN   **COOKING TIME** 20 MIN   **SERVINGS** 4

## Ingredients

- 1 pound raw potatoes, peeled and grated
- ½ pound cooked potatoes, mashed
- 1 egg
- ½ cup flour (more as needed)
- Salt to taste

## Instructions

1. Grate raw potatoes and squeeze out excess water. Combine with mashed potatoes.
2. Add egg, flour, and salt. Mix until a dough forms.
3. Shape into small balls or ovals. If desired, fill with sautéed mushrooms or minced onion.
4. Boil in salted water until they float and cook for 3-5 more minutes.

**Notes:**

- Storage: Store in an airtight container in the refrigerator and consume within 2 days. Freeze in a single layer for up to 3 months.

Chapter Twelve

# Regional or Oess Common Christmas Dishes

# SZCZODRAKI

Szczodraki are traditional Polish pastries often enjoyed during festive seasons like Christmas and New Year's. They are sweet, crisp, and symbolize generosity and good fortune for the coming year!

 PREP TIME **25 MIN**   COOKING TIME **15 MIN**   SERVINGS **12 PIECES**

## Ingredients

- 2 cups all-purpose flour
- 1 packet (2¼ tsp) active dry yeast
- ¾ cup warm milk
- ¼ cup sugar
- ¼ cup melted butter
- 1 egg
- ¼ tsp salt
- Optional: poppy seed filling or fruit preserves

## Instructions

1. Dissolve yeast in warm milk with a teaspoon of sugar. Let it sit 10 minutes.
2. Mix flour, remaining sugar, salt, egg, and melted butter. Add yeast mixture. Knead until smooth.
3. Let the dough rise for 1 hour. Divide into balls. Flatten, fill if desired, and shape into rolls.
4. Let rise again for 20 minutes. Bake at 375°F (190°C) for 15-18 minutes.

**Notes:**
- Storage: Store in an airtight container in the refrigerator and consume within 3 to 4 days. Freeze for up to 3 months.

# KIEŁBASA Z GROCHEM I KAPUSTĄ

Kiełbasa z Grochem i Kapustą is a hearty and traditional Polish dish often enjoyed during festive times like Christmas and New Year. It combines smoky sausage with peas and sauerkraut or cabbage, symbolizing warmth and prosperity for the family during the holidays.

 **PREP TIME** 15 MIN    **COOKING TIME** 1.5 HR    **SERVINGS** 4 - 6

## Ingredients

- 1 pound kiełbasa sausage, sliced
- 1 cup yellow split peas, cooked
- 2 cups sauerkraut, rinsed and chopped
- 1 onion, chopped
- 2 tablespoons oil
- Salt and pepper to taste

## Instructions

1. Sauté the onion and sausage until browned.
2. Add sauerkraut and cooked peas. Simmer together 20 minutes.

**Notes:**

- Storage: Store in an airtight container in the refrigerator and consume within 3 to 4 days. Freeze in a sealed container for up to 2 months.

# KUTERNOGA

**Kuternoga is a traditional Polish festive dish, especially popular in rural areas during Christmas. It's a rich and hearty pork roast slow-cooked with spices, symbolizing warmth and family togetherness during the holiday season.**

 PREP TIME **20 MIN**   COOKING TIME **1 HR**   SERVINGS **4 - 6**

## Ingredients

- 2 cups cubed dry white bread
- 1 cup ground poppy seeds (soaked)
- ½ cup milk
- ¼ cup honey
- ½ cup raisins or chopped dried fruit
- 1 tablespoon butter

## Instructions

1. Soak bread cubes in warm milk.
2. Mix in ground poppy seeds, honey, and fruit.
3. Spread in a greased dish, top with butter.
4. Bake at 350°F (175°C) for 25-30 minutes.

**Notes:**

- Storage: Store in an airtight container in the refrigerator and consume within 3 to 4 days. Freeze in a sealed container for up to 2 months.

# Conclusion

You've reached the final page of this cookbook, but we hope it's just the beginning of something far more meaningful—a tradition revived, a memory sparked, a new ritual formed around the kitchen table. Whether this is your first Wigilia or your fiftieth, whether you're Polish by heritage or simply by heart, whether your pierogi came out perfect or looked like small folded envelopes of love—what matters most is that you showed up, that you cooked with care, and that you invited others to join you in something beautiful and deeply human.

This book began with one woman—Babcia Wera—and her sixty-year tradition of making Polish Christmas dishes not just with skill, but with soul. Her recipes, carried in her hands, lived on in the quiet rhythms of her cooking, in the gentle murmur of boiling water, in the scent of cabbage rolls warming in the oven, in the sacred hush of Christmas Eve just before the first spoonful of soup was served. Over the decades, she fed more than stomachs. She fed hearts. She fed memories. She fed generations.

And now, through you, those traditions continue.

If you've made even one dish from these pages, you've joined a story far bigger than a cookbook. You've entered a living tradition, one that spans continents and centuries, one kept alive through shared meals, family laughter, a child's flour-dusted fingers, or the quiet tear of a grandparent watching a younger generation master a recipe they once thought might be forgotten. You've folded more than pierogi—you've folded in love, time, intention, and a link to the past that becomes a gift to the future.

Food, at its heart, is storytelling. The dishes you've prepared tell a story—not only of Babcia Wera and the Polish families who came before her, but of you and your family now. The act of choosing to cook these recipes, to embrace the slowness, the patience, and the care that traditional Polish cooking requires, says something profound in a world of fast food and rushed holidays. It says: this matters. We matter. Our stories, our roots, our connections—they matter.

You see, Wigilia is more than just a twelve-dish meatless feast. It's more than barszcz and uszka, more than herring and compote, more than poppy seeds and honey. It is a ritual of memory and meaning. Every bite carries symbolism. Every dish echoes centuries of faith, community, and resilience. And every seat at the Wigilia table is a reminder that we are not alone—that even the empty chair, set aside for an unexpected guest or a loved one lost, tells a story of inclusion, of grace, of welcome.

What Babcia Wera understood intuitively is something we've come to recognize with age: that food, lovingly made and intentionally served, becomes sacred. It is the language we use when words fail us. It is how we say, "I remember you," or "I love you," or "You are home." It is how we heal. And at Christmas, when the world quiets just enough for us to listen, that food speaks louder than any carol.

In every family, there comes a moment when tradition must be passed down. That moment is often quiet—just a hand guiding another over a bowl of dough, or a voice saying, "Watch closely—this is how my mother did it." In writing this cookbook, we've attempted to capture that moment and offer it to you. Not as a rulebook, not as a set of inflexible instructions, but as an invitation. We invite you to step into your kitchen with confidence, to try these recipes, to adjust them if needed, to burn a few things along the way, to laugh, to taste, to remember because this is how it has always been.

We hope that these recipes felt approachable and real. We designed them with modern home cooks in mind—whether you live in a city with Polish delis and access to traditional ingredients, or far from anything familiar, making substitutions with what you have. What makes these dishes authentic isn't perfection. It's intention. It's the hands that make them. The stories they carry. The people who gather around them.

And if, as you cooked, you found yourself remembering your own grandmother, or your father's quiet hands slicing mushrooms, or a family friend who once brought poppy seed cake to every gathering, hold onto those memories. Let this book be a bridge between where you came from and where you are. Let it become a journal of traditions restored, or new ones born.

It's possible that this is the first year you've tried celebrating Wigilia. Perhaps you grew up with bits and pieces of Polish culture but never knew how to pull it all together. Or perhaps the traditions had faded, lost through immigration, distance, and time. If so, let this be your new beginning. Let this be the year you made barszcz from scratch, the year your children learned to fold pierogi, the year your kitchen smelled like sauerkraut and mushrooms and something older than language.

On the other hand, if you've celebrated Wigilia for decades, we hope this book has served as a companion. A reminder. A warm echo of your own family's recipes, with some new ideas woven in. Maybe you tried a dish you hadn't had before. Maybe you found your grandmother's kutia mirrored in Babcia Wera's version. Maybe you read the introduction and saw your own family's history between the lines. If so, then this book has done what it was meant to do.

This is more than a book. It is a vessel. A preservation of legacy. A love letter written in flour and butter, in mushrooms and beets, in whispered blessings and the clink of opłatek wafers breaking between hands. And if it has touched even one holiday table, if it has helped even one family reconnect to their heritage or find joy in a new tradition, then every hour spent crafting it has been worth it.

We also hope this book has encouraged you to slow down. So much of today's world is rushed. Meals are grabbed, not made. Holidays are stressful, not sacred. But when you immerse yourself in these recipes, you cannot help but pause. You must soak. You must stir. You must wait. And in that waiting, something happens. Your kitchen becomes holy. Your time becomes meaningful. The chaos quiets, and what remains is what matters: the people around you, the stories you tell, the traditions you choose to keep.

And this is where your story becomes part of ours. Because every time you open this book, you become part of the circle. You bring Babcia Wera's legacy to life. You ensure that her sixty years of Christmas cooking weren't just something we remembered—but something that continues, multiplies, expands into kitchens we've never seen and families we've never met. That is the miracle of tradition. That is the beauty of shared memory.

When Babcia Wera made these dishes in the early days—before the internet, before modern appliances, before her recipes were written down—she wasn't thinking of legacy. She was thinking of feeding her family. Of honoring her own mother and grandmother. Of creating something warm in the coldest part of winter. But now, looking back, we see what she built. A generational feast. A sanctuary. A ritual of gathering that outlived change, displacement, and time.

So now it's your turn. To light the candles. To set the table. To share the opłatek. To tell stories. To cook slowly. To pass plates and pour tea and remember those who are no longer there. To make room at the table for those who need a place to belong.

We encourage you to write in this book. To make notes. To mark your changes. To write in the margins what worked and what didn't. To jot down the names of those you shared each dish with. Let this become your family's book, too. A living record of your own Christmases, of laughter shared and memories made. Because one day, someone else may open it and see not just recipes, but the story of who you were, of what you loved, of how you kept tradition alive.

Let this be the beginning of your own sixty-year journey. Let your children grow up with the smell of mushroom soup in the air. Let them know what it means to break bread, not just as a formality, but as a ritual of love and blessing. Let them learn how to fold pierogi beside you, not perfectly, but joyfully. Let them hear the stories of where their family came from, how they cooked, how they celebrated, how they loved.

And let it all begin with you.

To every person reading this conclusion, we thank you. Thank you for honoring these traditions with your time, your hands, and your kitchen. Thank you for bringing Wigilia to life in your own way. Thank you for helping carry forward a story that began long ago and still has many chapters to come.

We leave you with this blessing: May your hands be steady and your heart full. May your meals nourish body and soul. May your home always have room for one more. And may you never forget that even in the smallest acts—boiling a pot of soup, folding dough, lighting a candle—you are part of something sacred and eternal.

Wesołych Świąt.

And welcome to the family.

www.ingramcontent.com/pod-product-compliance
Lightning Source LLC
Chambersburg PA
CBHW082012030526
44119CB00065B/753